To the sm[...]
and we're glad we
have him!

Mom, Susan
and
Brian & Sargent

SMART DADS I KNOW

SMART DADS
I KNOW

DR. CHARLIE SHEDD

SHEED AND WARD, INC.
Subsidiary of Universal Press Syndicate
NEW YORK

Library of Congress Catalog Card Number 75-30

ISBN: 0-8362-0612-6 (cloth)

Contents

Introduction

"THE DIFFERENCE"

Fathering these days is on the way. It's on the way "in." Big city, small town, country—often and everywhere I find them. Dads with a real thing about being good dads.

What turned me on to this was an unusual experience on the way to Los Angeles. We were high in the sky and total strangers. Side by side. Reading.

He was reading an article on teens and the drug scene. With pictures. Horrible.

Suddenly, turning away from his magazine, the young man looked right at me. I had the feeling he really wasn't seeing me. He seemed to be looking down the road as he whispered from far down inside. Almost like a prayer he whispered,

"God, I wonder why? I suppose nobody knows. But if a father can make the difference, I sure want to make the difference."

So we took it from there. He gave me his card. I gave him mine. He was a salesman. Wife and three children. Fantastic job. Great company. Going up fast. A high motivation man. But nothing higher on his agenda than this—to make the difference as a dad!

You think it was a chance meeting? I don't. I think he did a good thing for me. He set me thinking. This kind of sharing from a total stranger always sets me thinking.

Ever since that day I've been doing a survey. I've been picking up on other men getting it together. And I find a lot of them.

Why is it happening, this gradual turn around to a more serious kind of fathering? Nobody knows for sure all the answers to a question like that. But isn't it amazing how one man's negatives can become another man's positives?

Early pregnancies. Drugs. Kids in trouble so many ways. They do turn us around. And in the retake we see some other things. Like? Like the rat race isn't really where it's at. Like people matter more than things.

These things I see and I think they're beautiful. More and more dads are taking their place where it makes a difference. That's what this book is about.

CHARLIE SHEDD
Jekyll Island, Georgia 1975

1

"Work-Aholic" Dads

"He's a 'work-aholic'!" That's one of the mod words for a guy who doesn't know when to quit. Hard charger, heading for another million. Scrabbling, clawing to the very top. Meanwhile, back at his address, the family grows up without much fathering.

Then there are others who would like to be home, but can't. Here's one dad who writes because he's worried.

Dear Dr. Shedd:

I'm writing because I'm in a trap and don't know what to do about it. Every week I leave home early Monday morning and can't get back until Thursday or Friday. There's nothing I can do about this for at least two more years. Maybe three. Sure, I could quit my job, but to tell you the truth the future looks great for me if I make it in this assignment. I don't know any company where I could do as well or any job I'd enjoy more. Yet my family really does mean more to me than my job. I thought you might know of some dads who have this problem and how they handle it. I'd sure be grateful for some help.

He wrote to the right place, because I know Emmett. He travels too, and he's one of the best fathers I know. He's also home only on weekends, sometimes Thursday, usually Friday. His wife is bananas about him. His kids think he's great too. All of which is no accident. He plans his weekend carefully.

So what does he do? He gives each of his children one hour alone with him.

Emmett says, "Sometimes I just sit in their bedroom and we visit. We might go out to breakfast. Or shop for something they need. Play catch. Watch one of their favorite TV shows. But you can bet each one gets sixty minutes."

Then there's Sallye. She's a wonderful mother. But even a wonderful mother can be up the walls at the end of a week alone with her children. Only she seems to take it better than most women I know.

If you were to ask her how she does it, she would smile from way down inside and tell you about Saturday night. She and Emmett have a standing date on Saturday night. They go out for dinner. Dinner and dancing. Dinner and a show. Dinner and shopping. Dinner and one of their favorite drives.

You can imagine how Sallye feels when Emmett tells her, "There is no social engagement, no company to entertain, no friend to visit, as important as being alone with you."

Sunday after church they have a big dinner. And a family council. They talk over important matters. Settle disagreements. Make decisions.

But when does the poor guy have time to do *his* thing?

Ask him and he'll tell you, "Sometimes I can get in a round of golf. But if I miss it, I can do that later. Right now my family comes first."

Recently Sallye said an interesting thing. "You know," she mused, "even if Emmett does travel, I think I get more attention on the weekend than most of my friends get all week." And I'll bet the same could be said for Emmett's kids.

2.

Taking the Kids Off Her Hands

Jerry is an optometrist. Young. Launching his practice in a small Southern city. Doing very well, because he's a good manager. He's remodeling his office with his own hands. Does most of it on his days off. Except now and then he drives a nail or two when he's not too busy seeing people.

I happen to know about Jerry, because I went to him for prescription sunglasses. We were going on vacation, so there was a deadline to meet. And he met it. Called on Saturday, told me he'd bring the glasses by if I'd be home.

He came looking for all the world like a tired hod carrier. Guess he'd been doing some plastering. But the dirt and the weariness were not what I noticed first. It was his three little girls. Chery is eight. Lisa and Lori both six. The thing you would notice about Jerry's daughters is that they are stunningly beautiful.

When you can see them. That Saturday afternoon you couldn't. Dirt, plaster, paint in layers. Several layers. And tired? Tired like only little girls get tired.

Jerry excused himself for his appearance. He asked the little girls to please wait outside on the porch swing. (Thanks, Jerry.) But I got the distinct feeling that he wasn't apologizing, just explaining. Then he grinned his boyish grin and said, "I told Judy to take the day off and go to the beach. She's been working too hard, needing a break. We had a great day at the office. Besides I think it does a woman good now and then to have a whole day without the kids."

So right. How do I know? One way I know is that I saw them at church Sunday morning. I wish you could have seen them holding hands. The way she looked at him, you would have felt what I felt—this is one warm love.

Plus, here's another good bet. What's going on inside those girls from a day with their dad is building good vibrations. Lots of good vibrations between three little girls and their father. Plus, the good vibrations kids get from good vibrations between their mother and dad.

One further note from another mother. I called my wife to come see the girls. Then when I told her I was writing a chapter on Jerry and his daughters, she said, "If you have room, put this in too. There are times when a woman especially appreciates a man like that. One of these is taking the children off her hands when she's getting ready for company."

Some kind of a "super special," isn't it?

Good dad, good husband. Good deal.

3

How Much Should a Parent Help with the Homework?

How much should a parent help with the homework?

Here's a father writing to get a few things off his chest.

This dad's daughter won first prize in a recent junior high science fair. Some kind of miniature computer, and from his description of the competition it had to be good. Only now the whole thing has been getting to his conscience. Here's one paragraph from his letter:

> This morning while I was reading the paper over coffee, it hit me. I was thinking about all those indictments in Washington. Reading my favorite editorial writer, musing on dishonesty. Cheating. And what's the world coming to. That's when it hit me. This science fair was a pure fake. I built that damn computer. What am I teaching my daughter? How to be a phony? I talked it over with a friend of mine. He said forget it.

19

But it still bothers the hell out of me. What do you think?

I think he's beautiful. Personal honesty is always beautiful. And boy, is it needed! All over the place it's needed. Including our parenthood.

Homework may be a good place to begin. A friend of mine teaches high school physics. He's been leading a crusade to do away with this kind of competition. Here's a part of his argument before the school authorities:

"The dullest boy in my class won first prize for his perpetual motion machine. It really was a classic. I couldn't believe his father was that smart either. So I did some checking and here's what I found: they paid a graduate engineering student to make it for them. Now what's any high schooler going to learn from that except how to cheat and get away with it?"

Good question. Only one answer.

So my friend is beating a loud drum. He's against any kind of school contest where kids can enlist parents to compete, family against family. And he does have some terrific arguments.

Yet, what do we do when our child says, "Will you help me?"

This is what we did in our family. Like other parents we've gone through it with all five of our kids and with our conscience. So we came up with a decision agreed to by all of us. For our family it's been a good deal and here's how it goes:

"We'll help with your homework on this basis: you

tell your teacher that you and your parents are working together. As long as it's O.K. with the school, it's O.K. with us. But remember we're helping *you*. Not vice versa."

Here's an interesting little addition. We've never had one teacher object to that.

4.

Car Discipline

What do you do when you're on a trip and your kids are fighting?

Closeness is beautiful, but sometimes it gets a bit heavy. Days when we're all cooped up; weeks when we've been seeing nobody much but each other. These "here we are together" times take some special handling. Maybe the poet had something when he said, "Let there be spaces in your togetherness."

So here's a dad's quiz on car discipline. You're taking a trip together and the kids are fighting in the back seat. They've been at it long enough now and it's time to blow the whistle. You've had it.

Options:

1) You speak to them in your sternest voice. But it doesn't work, so you shout. Success. Two minutes and twenty seconds of success. Then they're at it again. This time their mom screams. Same result. Strictly temporary. Conclusion: for long-range control "hollering" is not where it's at. So you move to number 2.

2) You stop the car and clobber them. Show them

who's boss. Only now you've got to listen to them cry. Plus, you don't feel so good inside. Loss of your self respect? Whatever it is, you know this—you've traded their fighting for some very uncomfortable feelings. Then how about number 3?

3) You turn the car around and announce, "We're going back home. I am not putting up with this any longer!" Of course, you don't mean it, but you're getting desperate. Yet this could be a double-whammy. You might be playing, "Cut off my legs and call me shorty." Maybe this particular trip is one you don't want to scrub. So move on to number 4.

4) You separate the kids. Some up front. Some in back. And then you add, "You better stay put if you know what's good for you." Improvement? Maybe, unless there's a big fight about whose turn it is to sit up front.

You're probably thinking, "I hope we'd be doing something better than any of these options. We'd bring along toys, color books, puzzles. We'd invent games. Sing songs. Or if we'd been in the car too long, we'd stop so they could run."

One dad I know came up with a different solution. He says, "When my kids get to fighting in the car, I just drive over to the side of the road, stop, turn around, and say, 'Hey, guys, do me a favor, will you? You're bothering my driving and I want to get you there safe. I'd sure appreciate it if you'd knock it off.'"

He says it works.

Do you suppose our kids would behave better if we talked to them more like adults?

Telephone Rules

The telephone can be a father-problem. Mother-problem too. And same for the young fry.

But here's one family who turned it into a good thing. I was a guest in their home, and we were sitting by the fire, deep in some warm conversation. Then came their daughter and said, "Dad, I've got to make a telephone call. This one will take a while. Do you have any important calls coming in?" When her father had given her the green light, she thanked him and ran along.

I thought that was something special. Extra special for a teenager. So I said, "You've got a winner there. Very unusual." To which her dad replied, "Thanks. But actually, it's all part of our deal. The telephone used to bug us. So we had some discussions and decided on a few rules. Everybody put in his two cents worth and then we voted. One thing we agreed was that we'd check with each other before a long call."

I know this dad well. He makes his living as a manufacturer's rep, and sometimes he gets important calls at the house. I asked him to clue me in on some more of their good stuff.

Rule Number 2: No eavesdropping. Short rule, but a real vacuum sweeper for hostility. All of us, adult and children alike, resent intrusion on our privacy. This is one of the major gripes I get from the young set. From junior high through the college crowd, they hate nosiness.

Rule Number 3: Homework comes first. Assignments are to be finished before any phone calls. Or, if it's a call coming in, get it over with fast and then back to the books.

Here's a little extra with a big plus. Homework can be done by phone if no one else needs the phone. But the important thing is trust. Everyone is on his honor.

For my money, this is quality living. These people have settled some of the problem areas ahead of time. They're using what could be trouble to bring them closer together.

Another dad I know made this deal with his kids: "When you begin to earn money (baby-sitting, carrying papers, anything) if you want your own phone, if you can pay half the cost every month, as long as I can afford to, I'll pay the other half."

For them it's been simply super. I guess it would be more accurate to say it's been super for three out of the five. Two wanted no part of spending their hard-earned money that way. But their mother and I thought it was a good deal even for them. At least they knew we were ready to go when they were.

He Takes the Big Shots Home
for Hamburgers

Did you see this bedtime cartoon? Mother sitting on shaggy rug with little ones. "Your father, children, is six feet tall. Handsome. Cute little mustache. Driving like mad to be vice-president, and he simply adores golf."

Funny. But maybe it isn't. Many a dad on the up-swish becomes a total stranger to his family. But I know of some who won't settle for that. Like John B.

John B. is on his way up. He's already gone a long way, but he's still going on up. He's president of a bank and on the board of directors for several corporations. He counsels, advises, invests, and makes decisions affecting many people. That's John B.

But when it comes to entertaining out-of-town executives, he has a different approach. Even the biggest wheelers and dealers among his acquaintances get the treatment. They know John won't take them out for an evening of drinks and dinner. Instead, he invites these honchos for hamburgers around the pool with Rachel and the children.

John does this for a very special reason. He's nuts about his family. So three years ago he made a decision. He said: "I was getting ulcers. The kids were getting complexes. Rachel was getting lonesome. And we were all getting way off base."

He told me this one night when we had been invited for hamburgers by the pool. Lots of food. Lots of talk. Musing on lots of things, and then he came on strong with this:

"One night in a hotel I was reading in the Bible when I came on this verse, 'What shall it profit a man if he gain the whole world and lose his own soul?' Right then I decided to get the family back in their right place on the agenda. That's why I bring these guys home. At first I wondered if it would hurt my business. Funny—things actually went better. As a matter of fact, I've made some awfully big deals by this pool over the hamburgers."

But that isn't all he's made. He's made some people think.

One of John's friends, a really big tycoon of the business world told me: "I get so damn tired of being entertained in fancy restaurants and bars. I love these evenings with John and his hamburgers and his family. I'm going to start doing it myself."

And here's another plus. I know John's three children well and I know what they think of him. And they say they've learned a lot from meeting these VIPs.

Especially Bruce and Steve. They're ninth and tenth graders.

Then there's Rachel. As I watch her with John, I can't help feeling, "There isn't a man alive who wouldn't like to get a woman that turned on."

So many good things come from putting the family first.

7.

Rap Three Times on the Back Door

Do you sometimes feel you're too busy? Too busy for all you'd like to do? Too busy for fun? Too busy for the things that matter—like being a good dad?

I recently heard of a doctor who did something about this. He was a small town doctor. Snowed with people problems. Physical. Mental. Heavy stuff and trivia. But his biggest concern was that he had two little boys and he wanted very much to be a good dad. So he made them a deal. He said, "Listen, *any* time you need me for anything important, you come and rap three times on the back door of my office. I'll be there as fast as I can make it."

The reason I know the story is that one of his little boys told it to me. He's a grown man now. And what a man! Dr. Gene Nida is head translator of the American Bible Society, World Bible Society, and United Bible Societies of the World. He supervises transla-

tion of the Scripture into over one thousand languages. Probably knows the Bible as well or better than anyone from anywhere. Brilliant. But warm and loving too.

I can't help wondering. How much of this man's brilliance comes from that little back door ritual? A growing boy can think better if he isn't wondering, "Does anybody care?"

And is his warmth traceable to the same origin?

I know another father who did an interesting thing when his daughter was growing up. And the really tough side of the story is that he was raising his girl alone. Yet he got the job done. I know how she's turned out. She's a grown woman now. I thought you might like this paragraph from one of her letters:

> When I started school, my father gave me ten cents and when he gave it to me, he said, "Patty, I want you always to keep this dime in your purse. Any time you need me, you call me at the plant. Tell them you want to talk to your dad, and I guarantee they'll let you right through." There is no way I could tell you what that ten cent piece from my father meant. Even when I didn't need him, just to know I had it in my purse made me feel secure.

Isn't it amazing how the little things can make such a big difference.

8

Too Successful?

Can a dad be too successful? For his kids' sake, can he over-succeed?

Here's an unusual letter from Detroit. This dad is obviously way up there. From his letterhead, his title, from what he says about himself, he's riding the top wave.

So what could be bugging him?

Nothing. He just wants to pass along one of his ideas. He suggests a column on making sure your kids can beat you at something.

Dear Dr. Shedd:

So many of the men in our company are having serious problems at home. We know it's part neglect. Too much business pressure. Not enough time with the family.

But I have another theory. Particularly, I see the sons of successful fathers get discouraged. When there's no way to improve on the old man's track record, why try?

You asked for ideas so I thought I should pass this along. We're raising four sons, and I'm making sure each one can do a lot better than I can at something. I work at finding a game where they can win. Something they can do well that I can't. I think it's important for them to know they can improve on the old man somewhere!

Shortly after his letter came, I attended an interesting seminar. This was a meeting of young hot shots. So I decided to introduce this "let them beat you" theme. We batted it around. Pro. Con. And most in the "never-gave-it-a-thought" category.

But there was one new father who said a fine thing about his dad:

"I know what the man is saying because my father got all kinds of honors. But I think there was a different reason why it didn't bother us. Our dad had faults like everybody. And he let us know that he knew it. He even asked us to help him with them. I want to be like that. No matter how well I do, I want my children to know I'm real ordinary in lots of ways."

Good idea. Maybe I need to spend a bit more time letting them see the real me.

9.

The Blue Jean Wedding

How does a dad know when to stand his ground and when to give in? Important question! A lot of fathers are asking it. Permissive parenthood is a bad scene. But so is bowing the neck when we should give in.

So, how can we tell "just right" from too much?

Nobody knows all the answers. But today's nomination for the right kind goes to a Minnesota father. He's refusing to budge and he writes me to check it.

His daughter is being married in a big church wedding. Alice Ann will wear the traditional wedding gown. Her bridesmaids also. But the groom is something of a rebel. He seems to enjoy shocking the adult world. Besides, he hates to dress up. So he says he and his groomsmen will wear blue jeans. Jean jackets—clean, open collar.

It's a fashionable church. Not stuffy, but dignified. And Alice Ann's dad says he won't pay for the wedding if the boys wear blue jeans.

She's leaning on him. Hard. Comes down especially heavy with this favorite of the young set, "But don't you believe in everyone doing his own thing?"

This dad is no old fogey. He's a very respected man in town. Takes plenty of time for his family. And he's allowed room in his schedule for some extras. He serves on the church board, and he really believes what he believes.

Now he's refusing to give an inch. No way he will foot the bill if the boys wear blue jeans. And I think the way he delivers his message is a classic. In reply to Alice Ann's "Don't you believe in everyone doing his own thing," he answers: "You bet I believe in everyone doing his own thing. It's one of my basic beliefs. In fact, I believe in it so much that I believe in ME doing my own thing. And my thing is not to pay for anything which would embarrass your mother." Terrific. Touché. Right on.

Some of the young set would have us believe if we're over thirty, we've had it. Our ideas don't count anymore. Their generation has the corner on what's smart.

Sure, it's true they may be smarter than we were at their age. But we still have one thing they don't have yet. That is the wisdom which comes with experience.

So let's stick to our guns. Tell them what we believe. We don't have to be preachy or judgmental or nasty about it. But a lot of kids need someone who will be definite.

It's this additional whammy that Minnesota father was holding out for—*responsibility to others!* Say it again, dad: "You better believe it, baby. Do your own thing. But while you're doing your own thing, don't forget your responsibility to all the other people, including your mom."

10.

Alternatives to Spanking

At our house we don't believe in spanking. Early in our parenthood we took the pledge. We said to our small fry:

"Now hear this! We are through forever with swatting and switching and all general clobbering. There has to be a better way than bare hand on bare derriere. We don't know for sure what it is but we'll work out something together. And whatever it is, it won't be physical. So, we kid you not, if ever we start to hit, you run like crazy. We've gone temporarily out of our minds."

To which from the general public comes the chorus, "What are you, some kind of subversive or something?"

Whenever my wife and I talk on parenthood, this is the point where the egg hits the fan. Spanking is one of those borderline holies. "You must be putting us on!

Are you questioning the ancient rite of the laying on of paddle, belt, brush, or articles too numerous to mention?''

Parents have a good reason for defending spanking. They know that a permissive background is strictly no good. Where "anything goes," everything is soon gone, including character. With no boundaries for behavior, a child becomes confused. And miserable. So if we don't believe in physical punishment, what *can* we do?

Here are a couple of true stories suggesting some possible alternatives:

Missy wrote all over her bedroom wall with a bright red crayon. That would require some action, wouldn't it? Her folks thought so, and her dad reports, "We gave her a choice. She's already on an allowance, so she knows something about values and what money can buy. But this is the second time it happened, so we decided we had to do something. We gave her the choice of forfeiting her allowance or staying in the house all day Saturday."

Now what do you think? Is that too much of a decision for a four-year-old? Can a child so young be trusted to choose what's best for herself? Missy chose to forfeit her allowance. She's an outgoing child with lots of friends and a fun yard. To give up her money was hard, but it was easier than being alone.

Robbie is nine. He left his bicycle out in the street. For the following week it was locked up in the utility room. Their milkman had backed over it once and they had to buy a new wheel. But that didn't stop him. He did it again, twice. That's when his dad made this rule: "Next time you leave your bike in the drive, we'll lock it up for a week."

Is a week too long? Just right? Not long enough? What other things could they have done to make a believer out of their boy? Robbie's dad says, "Sure, it was a rough week without his bike, but he's never left it out again. Not yet."

Why does that kind of thing work? One answer is that any child responds better to any built-in kind of discipline. It's so much less demeaning than physical punishment. It preserves a lot of that all-important dignity.

So, here's the father question for today: Is all discipline, punishment, control at our house done from a solid platform of genuine respect?

They Pay Him
Forty Miles Per Hour

Let's hear it today for the Hendersons. They must be extra special people. At least they have some unusual things going—

We thought some of your readers might like to know about an automobile deal we have with our son. The day he got his driver's license, we made an agreement. For some time he's been babysitting his two little sisters.

So this is what we did. We told Tommy we'd pay him forty miles an hour. This means he can drive the family car forty miles for each hour of tending the girls. We furnish the gas and we put him on his honor about the mileage. Sure, he could have an accident, but we think it's good for a boy when he's in a car to know his folks are trusting him. Besides that (thanks to driver's education), my husband thinks Tommy drives better than we did, as teenagers. This forty miles an hour has gone so well for us, we wanted you to know about it. It really is a lot of fun for everyone.

41

What do you think, dad? Do your kids have better judgment about some things than you had in your teens? Could they be trusted more if we trusted them more?

If we can accept that, we can have a base for working together. We can make certain agreements toward which the whole family moves. Things which cause trouble in other homes can draw ours together.

Another family did it in a different way. They put together what they call their "Credo for Self Government." One agreement in their Credo was a car-deal between the dad and each child. Since they started it early, this gave the children something to aim for.

"By the time you are driver's license age, if you have proven your good judgment, and if you have saved half enough for a second-hand car, your mom and I will put the other half with it and we'll get you on wheels. That's the good news. And here's the bad news. You must also save enough for half the insurance, which I regret to report, will probably cost more than the car."

It really worked well for four sons and one daughter. And, with us, it was just like the Hendersons. The more we trusted them, the better it went for all of us.

Incidentally, along the way we've bought a lot of nice old cars. Every one, the salesman said, had been driven by a little old lady. As a matter of fact, she never drove it anywhere except to church on Sunday.

Thanks, fellows! But then there was that one exception. Guess the little old lady drove hers to the drag races on Sunday.

12.

Dennis Is a Genius with Bicycles

Dennis is a genius at fixing bicycles. Always has been a mechanical whiz.

In second grade some of his best friends were working for A's. Not Dennis. He was taking his scooter apart and putting it back together. By junior high his mind was constantly turning over with wheels, sprockets, hand brakes, ten speed drives, and all that good stuff. During his high school years, he made his spending money by fixing bicycles.

Educationally, Dennis bombed out. He simply wasn't interested. Nobody would have guessed that either, because his dad is a college professor. And his mother is dean of women in the same school. They come from a long line of educators, but all that book-ishness wasn't for Dennis.

Today he owns a bicycle shop and you should see it. Bikes all over the place. New ones. Used ones.

Broken-down ones waiting for his expertise. In case you're thinking that's no big deal, better do a retake. Bicycles today are big, big business.

The thing you'll like about all this is what his mother and dad said. While Dennis was still in high school, they told him, "Son, we'd really like you to graduate. But we're going to get off your back about grades and a good record and going to college. We're proud of the way you can do things we can't do. In fact, we think you're just great. So more than anything we want you to be you."

And here's something else his parents say—"We think the schools of tomorrow will care more about the child's ability to succeed where he can, not where his parents think he should."

Here and there across the country I see some interesting experiments going on in education. This isn't my field, so I can only say, "Here's a tip of the hat to the innovators." I have a feeling tomorrow's schools will major in the uniqueness of each child. Pouring entire classes into standard molds forgets one thing. God doesn't turn out his children on an assembly line. He specializes in the person, not people en masse.

Sure, some schools are doing this now. But how long will it be before the majority reach this high level? Nobody knows that answer for certain.

So what can we do meanwhile? We can do what the professor and his wife did. We can put our parental hammers away and root for them to become what God intended.

That really is some statement from two members of a college faculty, isn't it? "More than anything we want you to be you."

13

He's Driving His Son to School These Days

Roy is moving up fast in his company, headed for the top. Good dad, too—now. But according to his wife, that's rather recent. She wrote saying she'd like other fathers to know about Roy and Kevin.

Here are a few lines from her letter:

> I think Roy has wanted to be a good father. But you know how it is. When a man does well in his business, he has to give it so much time. Kevin is seven and a great little guy, only his dad didn't know it. Then my mother became seriously ill, and I had to be away from home for two weeks. So Roy took over, and one of the things he seemed to enjoy most was driving Kevin to school.

Nothing so unusual there. Lots of fathers take over in emergencies. But what happened after the two weeks has a different touch.

When he knew his mother was coming home, Kevin made a request. "Daddy," he said, "I like it when you drive me to school. You know, talking about all this stuff. Couldn't we do it all the time?"

The difference between great dads and all the ordinaries may be right here. The ordinaries say, "Well, I have to make a living, don't I? Can't do everything." But the great dad takes another look at his agenda. He asks himself what's really important?

So Roy did a retake. He decided nothing in the business world mattered more than the business of his family. He made the necessary adjustments, and according to this report he's stuck to it faithfully. Every morning now, when he's in town, he drives Kevin to school.

There's one more line from the lady's letter in which she added an interesting side-effect. It occurred to me some of our readers might be needing this kind of bonus.

> You wouldn't believe what happened between Kevin and Roy. Two of the nicest guys in the world have discovered each other. But that isn't the only discovery. I have some feelings for Roy I never had before.

Now isn't that something? There's an old adage that the way to a man's heart is through his stomach. True? Maybe. But not much question about this: Sometimes the way to a woman's heart is through her children!

14.

A Confident Young Man

Glenn Lewis is in real estate. Manager of several offices for a big company. He is also one of the finest young men I know.

Glenn is confident. He knows he can do things. And he does them well.

Why do some men show so much moxie early? While others flounder around, these characters are getting it together. Many reasons, I suppose. But one has to be the training they had at home.

When Glenn was a high schooler in Madison, Wisconsin, he had a little car. It snows hard in Madison and sometimes it freezes hard. There are lots of winter time accidents there and Glenn had one of them. He wasn't hurt. But his car was. In fact, it was creamed. So, being the kind he was, he called home. And his dad came pronto. Nobody got a ticket because nobody was at fault. It was just one of those winter happenings on icy streets.

Some fathers blow up in emergencies. They ask stupid questions, say things they don't mean, rant, rave, and make fools of themselves. But not this dad. He checked to be sure Glenn wasn't hurt. Then ditto for those in the other car. He calmly established that his son had done all he could. And then they went home, Glenn and his father together. I mean in his dad's car, of course, but a whole lot more together than that.

When they got home, they reported to the rest of the family, discussed it a while, answered questions. Then that dad did something I think is great fathering. "Glenn," his father said, "will you go get us a loaf of bread?" And he handed his son the keys to the family car.

Still snowing. Still icy. A son still a bit rattled after smashing his own little automobile. And here is this dad saying, "I believe in you. I trust you."

If you could see Glenn Lewis today with his beautiful wife and two little children; if you could see him in his role as an officer in his church; leader in his community; if you knew he was only twenty-eight, you'd say, "This is some kind of fine young man."

Sure, there are a lot of negative characters around these days. But there are some great young people doing their thing, too. And most of them were shaped that way at home.

15.

We Have a Signal
for Phone Interruptions

The other day I was on the phone when an unusual thing happened. My friend at the other end said, "Dicky, I got your signal. Give me another minute." Then we finished our business and hung up.

Now my name isn't Dicky. It's Charlie. So what did my friend mean?

Because this bugged me, I dialed the number again, and asked, "Hey, John, what's with this Dicky bit?"

He laughed. We kidded a bit, and then he gave me the background. Very unusual. Too far out for some families, but I thought it might be right on for others. This was his story:

"We have four children, and they were driving us nuts interrupting when we were on the phone. You know, 'Can I have a cookie?' 'Julie hit me.' 'Tracy has to go to the bathroom.' Things like that. We'd yell. They'd cry. And we would all feel lousy. So we had a discussion and agreed on a signal.

"Now any time we're on the phone and one of them has something real important, he can come and stand in front of us, put both hands on top of his head and wait till we've said, 'I got your signal.' That may sound kind of silly, but we like it."

Sure, it sounds silly. But sometimes the silly things can do a lot. Especially, if they have just a touch of humor.

Then too, these silly people may not be so silly for another reason. They've decided ahead of time how to meet certain loaded moments.

Here's an exercise worth a family runaround. Think back to the last time you had any kind of disagreement with anyone. Give it a careful analysis. (Of course, you wait till the heat is out of it.) What does this "cool" review show? Are there certain things you could have done that you didn't do? Were you, are you, willing to do your part to make things better from now on?

The clincher to my friend's statement covers that last item and I need these words too:

"Our Julie is thirteen now, and she's forever on that phone. So instead of yelling at her, we use the same signal. You'd probably laugh to see a couple of adults standing with their hands on top of their heads. But we told them, 'If it's good enough for you, it's good enough for us.'"

Sounds fair, doesn't it?

Maybe we'd all do better with some signals around here.

16

The Dad Who Refused to Buy Grades

Some parent traps seem to be set especially for dads. And one of these is bribery. Because the old man makes it, he's the one to pitch when you want some of it.

I spend a lot of time with the high school and college set. They're super sharp and I admire a lot of their thinking. But some of it is strictly a con job. So a wise father studies the parent traps and stays alert.

Here's the story of one dad who wouldn't be fooled:

Early in his sophomore year at college, the son wrote home:

Dear Dad:

My roommate's folks have promised him a sports car if he makes all "A's" this year. I think that is great. And I was wondering how about you doing the same for me? That way we could have some competition between us. He is a brain. But you know I've never had much trouble with grades when I wanted to study. So knowing that I would get a car would make me want to study more.

I bet I could do it.

What do you say?

Love, Bruce

Now, how would you react to a pitch like that? Being a man, you might go for it. "You're on! I'll call your bet." Quick take-up on a challenge is part of healthy maleness.

He's a smart kid. Whether he knows it or not, he's using a likely pitch. That's how they are these days. So brainy they can get to our vulnerable spots even without knowing that's what they're up to. Which is one more reason why it's smart for any dad to do a retake on his first impressions.

When this dad did a retake, he wrote back what I think is a classic:

Dear Bruce:

No deal!

When I was in school, making "A's" was a big thing. Now I don't think it matters all that much anymore. And do you know who sold me on that? *You* did. Especially your last two years in high school and your first year in college. You told me that so often, I honestly think you're right.

So if I buy you a car for making all "A's" and grades don't matter, somebody isn't thinking straight. Right?

Buying you a car for straight "A's" isn't right for another reason. The more I live the more I realize life's greatest satisfactions are not in things. They can't be bought. Real satisfaction is how we feel about ourselves. With a mind like yours, learning ought to be reward enough.

Of course, I've talked this over with your mother, and she asked me to add this note. We're already proud of you, and no grade card would ever change our basic feelings.

Good luck, Dad

Smart kid. With a head like his, he shouldn't have trouble making good grades ever. But that isn't where the grading should end. In my book that kind of fathering rates an A+ every time.

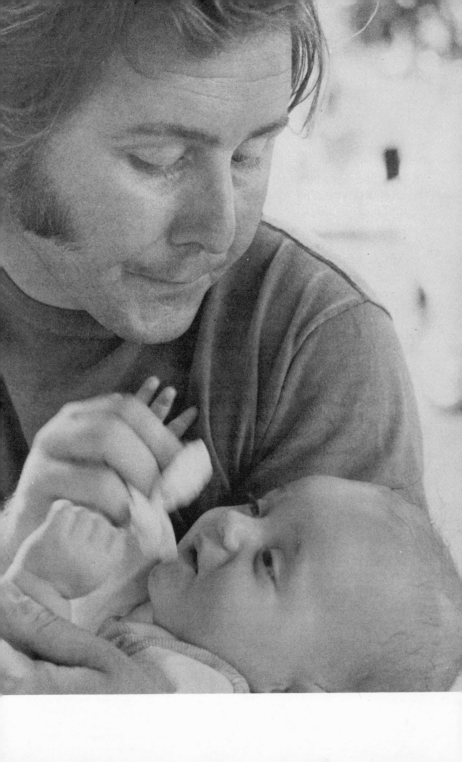

17

What Two Dads Said About Diapers

"You'll never catch me changing diapers. That's a woman's job."

This was Nick holding forth to the guys at the shop. Proud dad. Fine speech and he meant every word of it. He'd take his new son fishing, hunt with him, work on cars with him. He'd show him how to throw a curveball and the way to loft his jump shot. They'd camp and canoe. They'd do it all.

But changing diapers? No way.

Certain things are a mother's job. Women get used to stuff like that. Plus, shouldn't a baby be close to his mother for at least a year or two?

Lots of fathers feel like Nick. But is somebody missing something?

I once heard a baby expert, a woman doctor, present an unusual paper on the "Effect of Male Proximity to, and Relationship with, the Newborn Infant."

Which is one heck of a title for a very neat piece of information. What the lady said was that if the daddy is there, really there, he can make a walloping difference. She documented her arguments with charts and graphs. She was reporting on some studies she'd made. Studies on two sets of babies, and one group had this in common—their fathers were overseas.

Do you believe a baby is sensitive to his father's touch and smell and the sound of his voice? Sounds far out, doesn't it? But I've tried it on for size with other authorities, and they agree. One of them even made this startling claim—"In the not too distant future, we may discover that a newborn baby can pick up thought waves from the people around him."

I hope Nick gets close to his son later. Sounds like some great times coming. But wouldn't it be too bad if they both miss something they're needing right now?

Can a dad establish feelings in those first few months which he can never establish again?

Collin would say so. When they had their baby, he pitched right in. Sterilized bottles. Mixed formula. Fed. Burped. Rocked. Got up nights. Even changed diapers. No big thing, since it wasn't all the time. Collin works eight hours a day, and then some.

Yet Collin says, "I never saw anything like it the way this little guy grows. He actually responds and is it too much for me to believe we can really communicate?"

No, that's not too far out! And here's another thing not too far out. Maybe a baby responding like that to his dad makes for better response all around.

And that's not all. Nick's wife, I don't know. But Collin's, I do. She says, "I don't think anybody but a new mother can tell you how much a woman appreciates a helping hand with a tiny baby."

Do you suppose that had anything to do with this— Collin and his wife are one of the happiest couples we know.

18.

Heather's Father Changes His Mind

Bow your neck. Don't give an inch. Stand your ground.

Good advice sometimes. There are basic principles which we better hold to. Character is in part knowing what we believe and living by it. But sometimes for a dad, it isn't good advice. And the best kind of fathering knows the difference.

Heather is a high school senior. Gorgeous. The kind any dad would be glad to call his daughter. She works for him each summer. Receptionist. He says she's tops. Does an excellent job on the telephone and typewriter, but especially good with people. Even keeps some of his personal records. She takes the place of a regular employee.

Only her father has a rather unusual quirk. He doesn't believe in paying his own children. He says, "They work for me. I give them room and board, buy their clothes, pay their way through college. What could be fairer than that? That's the way my folks did it. Makes sense, doesn't it?"

Well, it didn't make sense to Heather. It bugged her to ask for money. So she sat her dad down and told him it was time for a retake. She was a big girl now. This year she wanted a different deal. He said it again: "But I don't believe in putting my children on salary. I've never done it. Nobody in our family has ever done it. Why should we change now?"

He shouldn't have asked it, because she had some answers. Nice, but straight to the target. "Dad, I think you're only burning incense to the past. Why follow an old family tradition that ought to be dropped right here?"

Then she came on with a proposal. "Tell you what, this year why don't you figure my time at regular rates? You put half of it in the bank for my education. Give me the other half to buy what you would be buying for me anyway. It wouldn't cost you one cent more than the way you're doing it. Besides I would get all that experience in handling money. You could watch and see how I do. Think how much better you'd feel when I go away to college."

That was one sharp proposition, wasn't it? In fact, it was so sharp her dad bought the whole package.

I admire young people like Heather. Brainy. Unwilling to settle for something just because that's how it's always been.

But there's another thing I admire. It's a dad who can change his mind when he should.

19.

He Hides the TV Tube

What do you think of a dad who hides the television tube? I mean he reaches into the set and takes out a tube so the kids can't watch. Sounds like some kind of ogre, doesn't he? But maybe the whole idea is worth a second look.

I know this father. I know his wife. I got the story from her, which means one thing for sure. She's a biased witness. I think the reason she likes him so much is that he's a "take charge" guy. Nice about it, but he's definitely a leader, and some women still do like it that way.

"The first time this TV thing happened," she said, "the kids were having a big fight over who could watch what."

Familiar scene? And these blow-ups always seem to come at the most inopportune time. Like when mother and dad are headed for an evening out together.

What she said in effect was that they weren't about to cancel in favor of peace at home. That's when father marched to the TV set and quietly removed a tube. No speeches. No threats. No arbitration.
    Action.

You know how well that went over. An evening of viewing each other is Dullsville when you've been counting on your favorite programs. You could lay bets on another thing. The thoughts they were thinking weren't exactly "We like daddy because . . . "

But popularity is a fleeting thing. Especially for a parent. Sometimes the small fry like us better when they view what we've done in retrospect. That's what happened here. I know because I talked with the kids.

But, let me tell you the rest of the story, which may help explain why it worked so well.

Of course it happened again, so the second time dad took out a tube, he said, "I will put it back as soon as *you* work out a schedule together."

Psychologists say that training in natural consequences is far superior to some of the old methods. "If you do this, you will get that." "If you don't do that, you will get this."

Why would this be more effective?

Today's young set is smart. No matter how old they are, they know a whole lot more than we knew at their age. But though they are smarter, we can still be wiser. So let's hear it now for all wise dads. I'm not arguing for removing tubes from the family television. I wouldn't even know where to find the right one in our set. Maybe you wouldn't either. But there are lots of ways to keep on top of things at home.

Here's a tip of the old sombrero for any father who can out-wise his smart kids.

20.

Why Jewish Children
Respect the Law

Letter from a juvenile judge in Pennsylvania. And he rattles my notions on first reading. But checking further I think he zeroes in on something important.

Dear Dr. Shedd:

Have you ever asked yourself why Jewish children are very rarely in trouble with the law? You do a little checking and you will see that what I am telling you is true. It is very seldom that a Jewish child is brought into my court. Also on the rare occasion when it has happened, someone in his family comes quickly to get it settled. Almost always when they come like this, the court can transfer the child immediately to his parents. In some cases to his grandparents. We can do this because we know the matter will not be treated lightly. As a matter of fact, they will likely settle it promptly and with dispatch.

Do you know why our Jewish children are so seldom involved with the law compared with other children? It is because our religion is family-centered. For us the synagogue is only an adjunct, an extension really, of the basic moral training which takes place in our homes.

Thank you judge, for your letter. Being a Protestant I didn't warm up quickly to your claim. So I decided to do my own personal survey. Result? Every juvenile court I checked said, "The judge is telling it like it is."

I suppose that's much too general to be true everywhere in the country. But since it's obviously true in many places, I decided to do some further checking.

I went to see Sam. He's one of my Jewish friends and very sharp. Successful merchant, plus an outstanding father.

So I asked him, "Sam, will you read this letter? If the judge is right, I want to do a write-up on what he says. Let's get specific. Tell me exactly what you folks do to develop that basic moral training at home."

He did.

He said that every week for years their family had a session on the law. He'd been raised that way. And he was raising his children that way too. So I asked him, "Would you mind getting specific about that too?"

"Of course not," he answered. "Right now we're having some lively discussion on the Ten Commandments. Marvin and Beth are both in college, you know. So we discuss all the new ideas they're getting on campus. We talk about morals and government, things we're reading these days, what we're seeing on television. I guess that's part of what the judge means by basic moral training. And he's absolutely right. We think the best place to get this job done is in the home.''

Thanks, judge, for a great idea! And you too, Sam.

21.

I Can't Leave Town
till the Baby Comes

Brad wasn't there when his son was born. The reason I know is that my wife and I were. We drove Carol eleven miles to the hospital. Rough ride. Every little bump must be a big one when the time has come to deliver. But it was also rough because Brad was two thousand miles away.

Her friends understood. They all pitched in. Took care of the two little girls. Visited Carol at the hospital. Sent flowers.

But there was one thing none of us could do. We couldn't substitute for Brad. When a new baby comes, the scene calls for a father. Who else will be pressing his nose against the window every 30 minutes? Smiling. Getting excited. Worrying a bit. Bragging. Holding the mother's hand. It wasn't that Brad didn't care. In fact, maybe he cared too much. He was off on the biggest deal ever. This one he couldn't miss. The president told him, "Brad, you nail that contract down and the sky's the limit for you."

Some companies do want men who will put their business ahead of everything. Brad figured it meant a bigger home, better living for the children, nicer things for Carol. She was a good sport about it. On the surface. But then she began to wonder. Are there men who make their woman number one on the agenda? And how would it be to live with a man like that? Well, she found out and I'll spare you the details.

Then there was Martin. He had a travelling job, too. Troubleshooter. Sold along with it, and did well for the company. And he did something else well.

Thirty days before their baby was due, he told his boss, "I can't leave town any more until after the baby comes."

You'd think even a high mogul could understand that. But this one couldn't. He turned all the screws—pressured, maneuvered, threatened. I know because I've watched the big man operate on some of his boys before. Only this time Martin stood his ground. He wouldn't go.

That was eighteen months ago. And it's been a tough eighteen months for Martin. But the other night we bumped into him and his family at the cafeteria.

I wish you could have felt what we felt when Nancy told us, "We're moving. Changing companies. Martin has been offered a wonderful job." Martin said "wonderful" might not be the word for it. He said his new employer had been one of his customers, so he knew what he was getting into. The business was in really tough shape and they were asking him to come straighten it out.

I suppose they know what kind of man he is. But whether they do or don't, Nancy does. She thinks there's nobody like Martin.

22

The Family Business Session

Three little boys bragging:

Druggist's son: "My dad makes more money than anybody. He gives these people a little bitty bottle of pills and they give him a whole lot of dollars and cents."

Number two: "My dad is a writer. He types up some stuff, takes it to the post office, and pretty soon we get a bunch of checks."

Preacher's son: "Aw, that's nothing. My father talks for twenty minutes and it takes twelve men to carry the money down the aisle."

It's an oldie. But the last time I heard it, something new happened in me. Suddenly, I was face to face with the question: How much *do* my children know about our family income? Do they have any idea where it all goes? House payments, insurance, utilities, contributions, food, clothing, automobile, gasoline. When they hear the word "inflation," do they have any basis for their comparisons? What do taxes mean in their heads? Savings? Could they possibly know how much it takes to cover miscellaneous expenses?

Today's nomination for one smart dad is Stanley Stanek. He's a factory foreman, from Ohio. Obviously a thinking father, and I have selected this single paragraph from his letter:

> At least once every three months, we have a family budget session. My wife and I sit down with our kids and lay it all out there. Big expenses and little. Then we discuss allowances and everyone has a chance to make his particular pitch. Know what I mean? New bicycles, the school formal coming up—things like that. We're real high on this at our house.

So are we. And if you haven't tried it, you'd like it. After you'd been at it, you'd hear your kids saying things to convince you. Here are some quotes from the young front where family business sessions are the thing:

"After I heard all about where it goes, I could see how it would matter more if I carried papers to earn some of my own stuff."

"Well, I guess maybe it makes a person understand why he can't have everything."

"It helps you to plan ahead when you want something. Then when you know everything, you don't mind waiting so much."

And I will not soon forget that session when one of our junior highers came with this classic. Suddenly, seeing the enormity of it all, he turned to me and said, "Gee, dad, take care of yourself."

23.

Teaching Our Children
How to Meet People

Recently I was in a crowd of the young set. As I approached one boy, he put out his hand and said, "My name is Tracy Spalding."

From there it was simply super! Great conversation! He told me a lot about himself, asked some things about me, and I think you would have been excited as I was with Tracy. Extraordinary. The average teenager is a sullen character. Non-communicative. Or if he does talk, the sound you hear is more like a mumble. And that's too bad, because all his life he'll be meeting people.

I really am high on teens in many ways. But most of them can vibe better with teenagers than they can with adults. Maybe that's natural, feeling as they do. Adults are creeps. Why bother?

Yet, here's Tracy doing his thing, putting out his hand. Asking some questions.

How does he get that way?

I spend a lot of time in the teen scene, so it's easy for me to ask questions. I can get answers straight from where it's at. So that's how I could ask Tracy: "Hey man, you've really got it when it comes to the old P.R. Where'd you learn to relate like this?"

"Well," he said, "mostly it was my dad. From the time I was little, he taught me to put out my hand and say, 'My name is Tracy. What's yours?' Nearly everybody likes it."

We talked some more about his dad and I came up with a couple of interesting items. This man works for a big oil company. One of his jobs is recruiting college students. He interviews seniors at private schools and state universities. He would know a thing or two, wouldn't he, about the importance of an outgoing personality?

And there was one line I remember word for word from Tracy's conversation, "My father always says they can hire all kinds of brains. But what he's really looking for is 'people-people.'"

Question: What am I doing to help my kids be "people-people"?

24.

Rally His Remaining Resources

"Say a good word." "Put in a plug." "Give an encouraging little nudge, won't you?"

Nobody but an author could believe the blizzard of requests. Dozens of eager beavers asking for help to herald their thing. Amazing how many special days, weeks, months are getting a push from someone— "National Raisin Week," "Strawberries and Cream Month," "Pancake Days."

Newspaper columnists aim their writing mostly to that 80 percent in the middle. But here's a mother and dad asking me to pass along one thought for parents of the handicapped. Good idea. Especially since their message applies in almost any home.

They're quoting a child psychologist whom they've heard lecture on the theme "Rallying the Remaining Resources." Here's the doctor's key phrase: "Your number one challenge as parents of the handicapped is

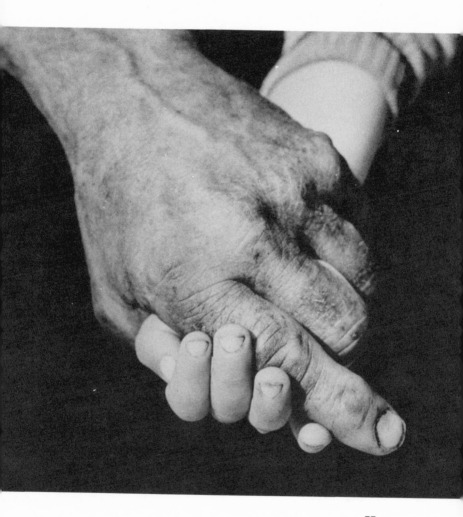

to quit concentrating on what your child doesn't have and rally his remaining resources."

Hardly one parent among us who doesn't need a touch of that. Most of us tend to become too pushy-pushy. Which, if we don't restrain ourselves, could be a real negative. Like this further bit of warning from the psychologist:

"If you attempt to make your child over from his basic nature; if you pressure him to achieve what he's not capable of achieving, you create a neurotic every time."

Here are excerpts from two more letters sounding the same theme: "My dad played minor league baseball and he thinks I ought to be a big leaguer. Now I like baseball, but what I really like is architecture. You know, buildings and bridges and things like that. Only I can't talk to him about this, because all he thinks about is me being a baseball player."

Letter two is from a dad whose son has just finished high school. "Hughie didn't finish at the top of his class and he didn't win any honors. But under his picture in the annual, they put, 'Hughie is a people guy.' His mother and I can't think of many things we'd rather have them say about Hughie than that."

Reminds me of a motto I saw in the library of a school for the blind. Written in braille, and under it, these words:

"It isn't what you don't have, it's what you do have that counts."

25.

He Can Navigate by the Stars

In twelve years they hadn't missed one day of school. It was a big class and only three of them had twelve years of perfect attendance. So these three were specially honored at the graduation ceremony. We gave them a big hand. And why not? Can't improve on perfect. Or can we?

As I was musing on this, I thought of the Howards. The Howards are big on togetherness. So big they'd rather spend time as a family than anything else. They go on trips. They play games. Or maybe they just sit around the table and talk. They've even been known to take their kids out of school for vacation.

Steve has an unusual job. He's locked into tourism, so he can't get away in the summer. He is also a sailing buff. Last year they decided to go sailing. They took a trip by boat with their whole gang as crew.

Each had his particular job. Work tailored to the age

of the children, but everyone essential. Steve said it was terrific.

This kind of thing raises some questions, doesn't it? And some eyebrows. Is it wise to take a child out of school for two weeks?

Well, what kind of student is he? That's a fair question. In this case, the Howard kids do fine—except Ricky. He's fifteen now and he's always had it rough.

Some of their friends thought the Howards were out of their minds. Naturally. We're all oriented to think of education as a number one priority.

But Steve Howard has never let criticism rattle his principles. He's a true conservative in some ways. In others he's an independent. But he does have a very definite set of values, and he trains his children that way.

One night shortly after their vacation, his friends were laying it on him. "What would the school do if every parent thought like you think?" Steve didn't have an answer for that. But even when they got on him about Ricky, he kept his cool.

He listened to all their lecturing on the importance of formal education. Then, when they'd finished, he said something that really bore down on me. "What IS education really? We all learned so much during those two weeks, and a lot of it about togetherness. And I'll tell you one thing Ricky learned. He learned to navigate by the stars. I wonder how many boys in his school know how to navigate by the stars."

Any dad these days with his head screwed on will not take education lightly. He'll respect the formal kind and the other kinds.

But he will also take a hard look at Steve's questions: "What *is* education really? *Does* anything matter more than togetherness?"

26.

Are We Doing Too Much for Our Children?

He is a Texas millionaire. Hit it big in the oil fields.

One night he called his five children, sat them down and said, "Gang, we're making a lot of money. Some of my friends and some of their kids have gone to hell down this road. But we're not going that route. I'm giving you notice right now that your old man will pay for one half of your college education. No more. The rest is up to you."

I know that dad. I know his family. And it was a very good deal.

It's always a good deal when any father can restrain himself from overdoing for his children. There is something innate in us which makes us see ourselves as the "protector." Unless we guard this, we could make a serious mistake. "Easier" is not necessarily better. Take away challenge, weaken character.

Some parents I know start the training early. Little jobs for little people. Then more responsibility as the child grows. Finally, they're ready for some of that Texas father's fifty-fifty dealing.

At our house one of the best agreements we ever made goes like this: "On the big things, you raise half the money. Work. Save. Plan. Dad will match you with the other half." For our bunch, it's been beautiful.

Almost any child will take everything he can get free. He will receive and receive and then he'll begin to wonder why he isn't receiving more. But it isn't doing what he thinks it's doing. It's not making him happier. And it isn't doing what we'd like it to do. It's not making him stronger.

Did you see the cartoon where a young employee is standing before the company president? Fine looking young man. And Mr. Big from behind his desk is saying, "I'm proud of you. Nobody has ever risen faster in the ranks than you've risen. Six months ago, messenger boy. Then office manager. Next, department head. Now vice president. Yes, I'm very proud of you." To which the young man answers, "Gee, thanks dad." Good for a laugh, maybe. But maybe it's sad. Some things in character can only be had by digging in. Long, hard digging.

One more time the question: Can a father do too much for his children?

And one more time the only answer: Yes, he can!

27.

Mountain Climbing over Mole Hills

Do you tend to fuss too much over trivia? I'm guilty. Sometimes I do make too much over too little. Here's a letter coming my way from a young businessman and right on target for our theme.

"Dear Dr. Shedd:

"Thought I'd pass along something my business partner told me. I feel like a better man since he told me. And I think my family likes me better too. What he said was, 'You'd save us so much trouble if you'd quit mountain climbing over mole hills.'"

Then he shows what kind of man he is with this admission: "I knew my partner was right when I thought over what he said. I was disagreeing with customers on every minor detail. You know what I mean? Didn't let them get by with a thing."

He signed his letter "Retake Ray." I like that. I needed his reminder. Most of us can use a retake now and then.

Right away, he said, things began to improve in their business. So much improvement in fact, he decided to try it at home. Being an honest man, he told the whole tribe what he'd learned, and asked them to give him a hand. Unusual approach. But excellent. Admit the problem, and solicit help.

I like the way he put this: "When I quit being a bloodhound for all the family's faults, they actually began doing everything better. I don't know what all goes on between a kid and his parents, but I know when I was little my folks were always nagging me. So I think I aggravated them just to fight back. I decided maybe my kids were doing the same thing. Anyway, relationships at our house have improved so much you wouldn't believe it's the same family. We're even having some fun—all of us together. And that's something new too."

"Fun." It's really great whenever a dad can turn things around like that.

Would the business of fathering go better if we lived by that businessman's advice? Perhaps this would be worth a frequent retake:

"We save so much trouble when we quit mountain climbing over mole hills."

28.

Time Together Alone

A dad in Des Moines, Iowa, did an interesting thing last fall. He knocked on his daughter's door one night right after she'd gone to bed. Then at her invitation he went in, sat down and made this little speech:

"Vicky, I want to apologize. I want you to know I'm sorry for a silly thing I've done. You're a senior in high school now. And all these years I've been saying that some day I'd take the time for us to get acquainted. So here you are with nine months left at our house. Then you'll be going away to college. And getting married. And Lord only knows how far we'll be from each other.

"So now I want to ask if you'll do me a favor. Once every week in this senior year, I'd like to take you out alone for a meal when we have time to talk together. I know you're busy lots of evenings and I can't get away for lunch. But maybe we can get up early once a week and go out for breakfast. Just the two of us, you and me. That's my invitation. Take some time to think it over and let me know how you feel.''

So she took some time. Like thirty seconds. Then she threw her arms around him. From there, he says,

it's been so fine. "What I've found out is that this is one great kid. It really feels good to know maybe her mother and I didn't do so bad after all."

Other dads from all over the country have asked for further information on a simple little practice we call "time out with dad." It began early. From the time our children were two, I took each one out every month for dinner alone. No big deal money-wise. They usually want a hamburger, pizza, spaghetti. But what they really want is that time with dad.

Once a month from two to college is about two hundred times. You can get to be best friends in that many hours. Nobody else—no phones, no door bell, nothing to steal a father's attention. Just the two of us, eyeball to eyeball.

We hear a lot about the generation gap. They won't talk. They clam up. All they do is grunt. Which is a very real complaint. What can we do about it? Well, there is one thing we can do about it. We can build our friendship before they barricade themselves. If we have given them the time prior to teen withdrawal, the old friendship is more likely to break through.

I think this background is especially important when it comes to sex education.

"Kids today just won't ask questions"?

Oh yes, they will! And the dad who offers his time often enough, long enough, knows they will.

So here's a hearty thanks to that dad in Des Moines, Iowa. I'm glad he wrote, because he answered another question I hear often: "When is it too late to begin?" He's telling us first hand that as long as they're still around, it's never too late.

29.

Goodness Is Its Own Reward

Overheard in an airport: "Now you be good, and we'll bring some presents." Obviously, mother and dad were leaving their children with the grandparents. And at the security check, they said it one more time. "Now you be good and we'll bring you some presents."

No way I could point a finger. I've done it. And if you have, welcome aboard. There must be millions like us. Nothing wrong with bringing presents. Builds happy memories. For me. For them. Most of us need all the good vibrations we can get. So let us come bearing gifts.

But why hook them up with good behavior? Why not? Here's one reason: If I gave my kids this treatment, and if they didn't outsmart me, I'd be ashamed of them. Soon they'd be saying—"*If* I'm good, what'll you bring me?"

But here's another thing wrong with this attempt to bribe for righteousness. Truth is I'm going to love my children whether they're good or not. And, I'd like them to know the truth of that old adage, "Goodness is good enough to be its own reward."

I also want them to know that happiness isn't in things. Prizes, surprises, accumulating—this isn't where it's at really. I know too many adults who operate under this delusion: happiness for them is material things. Even their people-dealing is tainted with the same philosophy: "What will I get out of this?" or "What have you done for me lately?"

One of the most interesting letters I've received lately comes right from the heart of this problem. An unhappy grandfather is unhappy with his equally unhappy son-in-law.

The old man writes: "When I started high school my father made me an offer. He said, 'If you don't smoke until you're twenty-one, I'll give you $100.' " (Remember the good old days when $100 was some deal?)

Now hear this: "So I made my two grandsons the same proposition. Only since money is not what it used to be, and I can afford it, I offered them $1000 each. I thought I was doing a good thing. But their father literally raised hell. He said if his kids don't smoke, it will be because they decide not to. It wouldn't be because somebody paid them. My wife thinks I should back off. But I say he's being unreasonable. We agreed I'd write to find out what you think."

Thanks for writing, grandpa. Having three grandchildren of my own, I can understand how you feel. But in this case, I've got to side with your son-in-law. I think this time he's the solid thinker.

That really is a fine old principle for fathering and for grandfathering:

"Goodness is good enough to be its own reward."

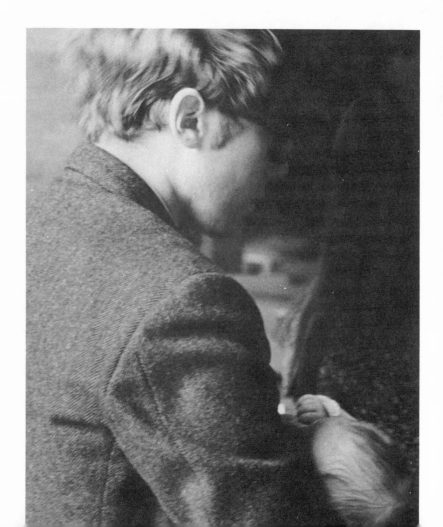

30.

Two Back Yards

The doctor has a new trophy for his azaleas. He's been raising prize azaleas a long time. He's also big on landscaping—bushes, special plants. You'd love his weeping willow and the neat blue spruce. And does he ever have a lawn! Groomed to perfection!

Only the doctor has a problem. His back yard backs up to Don's back yard. And Don's back yard looks like an amusement park, especially on weekends. Kids on the teeter totter. Playing in the tree house. Shooting baskets. Flying in the airplane swing. Romping over Don's obstacle course.

Don is a creator; he designed and built all of this stuff. He's a hobby craftsman. And any time he's working in his shop, the neighborhood kids all gather. You can hear them pounding, sawing, making things. Boats and planes. Houses and barns. Stilts, sundry items, and presents for their mothers.

Don keeps scrap lumber on hand, a supply of extra hammers, plus nails. He has a collection of saws, screw drivers, old cans filled with nuts and bolts. Hinges, hooks, string and wire. Paint brushes, too.

All the little people having their fun spill over sometimes on the doctor's show place. So the doctor isn't exactly enthusiastic, and I can understand. It does get noisy. Neurological surgeons have a right to some quiet. They're working on other people's nerves and it must get hairy.

Yet somehow Don and the doctor have managed to tolerate each other, back yard to back yard. Words, sometimes. But no law suits. A bit surprising maybe, since they've been living like this for years.

Perhaps the doctor senses some good from these goings-on. It is good.

I've had a chance to observe it close up. I've known a lot of those children trained in Don's workshop. And I've seen a bunch of them romp through his back yard playground to maturity.

I have a theory that anybody's boy or girl will come out better if he grows up with one bridge across the generation gap. Sure, it's especially nice when this can be a parent. But sometimes a substitute bridge can make the difference. As a case in point, here are Tommy, Patrick and Allison. They're really fine young citizens. Guess they would be. They spent more time with Don than anyone. That would be natural. Their back yard backs up to his back yard. Plus their dad was awfully busy, operating, landscaping, growing prize azaleas.

Test question for today:

In my fathering am I more like the doctor or like Don?

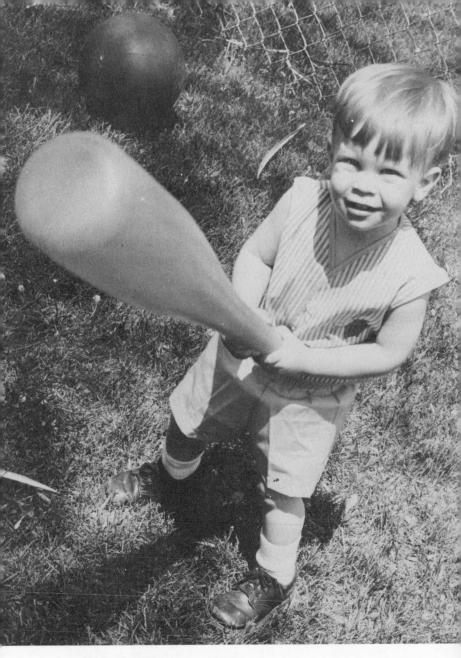

31.

The Big Lion

"There's a great big huge lion out in our yard."

That's what he said. Which might have been all right under ordinary circumstances. But this was the day of his mother's bridge club.

You know how it is. Sometimes with the public watching, you can't let certain things pass. Glancing out the window, she saw the neighbor's yellow cat. Large cat all right, but no lion.

"Warren," she said, "you know we don't tell lies at our house."

Then, with a bit of added flourish, she sent him to his room.

What else could she do with the bridge club watching?

Ordinarily, when we are wondering what people will say, we say too much. Which is exactly what she did. For whatever reason, she put on this extra touch:

"Maybe it would be a good idea, Warren, if you had a talk with the Lord about that!"

In less time than it takes to say, "Heavenly Father, Amen," the little guy was back.

"Well," said one of the extroverts, "that was quick. What did God tell you?"

"Oh," answered the grinning youngster, "He said, 'Don't worry Warren. When I first saw it, I thought it was a lion too.'"

Most of us would say she had it coming. Some things from the parent's side are better overlooked. Fantasy may be one of these. Given a normal home and a normal child, the make-believe normally takes care of itself.

Plain out and out lying may bear closer scrutiny. But even here things will go better with some elasticity. This is especially true in those early years. Before their sense of truth is well-defined, most small children will tell some whoppers. Much of this is experiment and it will pass. Gradually they learn that truth is the better choice. Better for everyone—for what others think of them; for what they think of themselves.

Almost any dad worth the name will say, "I want my children to grow in this direction. I want them to be honest, to respect the truth."

So how can we get the job done? Well, we can tell it like it is. Discuss it. But there is another way, and it's not easy. We can show them our own feet of clay and solicit their help.

One father I know found the courage to make this declaration: "Hey gang, I need your help. I want you to know that I know I'm not perfect. Whenever you catch me lying or cutting corners, I want you to stop me. You can do it decently, in private, but straight. I'll appreciate everything you can do to make me a better man.''

Would I dare come down off my father image like that?

Would you?

If we let our whole tribe see the egg on our face, what will they think?

To find the answer, I asked two of that father's children, ''When he told you he wasn't perfect, what did you think? How did that make you feel about your dad?''

To which I got these answers:

''I think it is neat, because you don't have to worry so much if you make a mistake. It is a good feeling to know you don't have to be perfect.''

''Funny how it works. It really doesn't make you think less of him. Instead you just think more of him than ever.''

32

A Million Is Never Enough

Is it ever right to get a divorce? You've heard that question often. So have I. Writers get letters from people with all kinds of problems. And those contemplating divorce somehow hit me especially hard. Like this:

Dear Dr. Shedd:

When is it right to break up a marriage? I had decided on divorce. Changed my mind. Decided again. But you can see I'm still wondering.

The problem is that he said when he made the first million, then we would enjoy life together. Now it's made and he wants two million. Do you know what I think? I think he has an incurable disease.

For some time now I've been watching this creep up on the children. They have so much, but they're never satisfied. What's troubling me is that this horrible thing which is destroying my husband might destroy them. Do you think it's possible to have so many things that you finally reach perpetual misery?

Yes, I think that's possible. I've known men who could write a check for almost anything. But they weren't happy. And they were operating under a delusion. It was the delusion that their next big deal would make them happy. Yet it never did.

I've known women whose mink covered a deep heartache. I've seen children standing knee deep in toys, unable to enjoy any of them. I've known young

people surfeited with things, asking, "So what else is new? Where's the fun?"

Who is to say when divorce is right? Don't look at me. My thing is to keep families together if there is any possible way. But who can blame her for wondering? Should the whole tribe be destroyed because their head man is a money maniac?

Yet money isn't the destroyer. It's the attitude. And some people turn their money into great living.

Like the Christensens. Successful farmers. Super successful. They own acres and acres of land. Houses, barns, cattle, machinery. They operate big.

Because they made it in agriculture, they want to help others make it. They have a cattle project going for 4-H boys on an Indian reservation. They've established scholarships for veterinary students of foreign lands. Sheep. Hogs. Seeds. Wells in the desert. A donkey project in Ecuador. All these things the Christensens are doing with their money.

Why?

Because their father trained them that way. He's out of it now. But the four boys aren't. Neither are their families. And I wish you could meet them. They are among the happiest people I know.

Effective fathering these days will include teaching how to earn, how to save, how to spend. But the best dads know something else. They know that sons and daughters need more than material things for total happiness.

And one thing they know for sure is training in how to give. That's the one sure guard against money-mania.

100

33

"Clean Your Plate" and Other Silly Traditions

Poor little kid! There he sits at the dinner table. Everyone else is long gone while he messes around with the food.

The problem? His dad. And I know because of this letter from his worried mother:

Dear Dr. Shedd:

Do you think a child must clean his plate at every meal? My husband has an awful thing about this. He says that's how his parents raised him and that's how we're going to raise ours. I'm not a waster. I know food is expensive, but honestly I'm worried. It seems to me we're creating some real problems. Like making him nervous and building resentment. Can you tell me anything that would help me help my husband understand?

You bet I can. I can tell you about another stupid dad—me.

I was raised on "clean your plate." So were a lot of other people. Only with me it really "took." Had it not been for Dr. Arrendell, I might be "hung up" yet.

I know nutrition is important. And I'm not arguing for a total lack of regulations. All of us need wholesome foods. There must be some family rules about sweets. A fistful of cookies before meals isn't good. The same thing goes for little green apples and cokes unlimited.

But one night at a church dinner I was badgering my own son to eat his plate clean. Easier to do silly things with your first child, isn't it? So his plate was piled high now and I was pressuring him to eat every bit of it.

That's when Dr. Arrendell spoke up. He was our family physician. A gentle man. So knowing. He had been watching us. When he had stood it as long as he could, he said: "Let me tell you something about boys. What you don't know is that God put them together so they understand better than you do how much food they need. Why do you want him to clean his plate?"

So why did I?

"Was I simply doing what my folks had done?"

"Was I worrying too much what people would think?"

When I did a thorough retake, I knew the doctor was right. My wife and I had been concentrating too much on what kind of parents we were. What we needed was a finer focus on who we were parents to!

Good fathering these days might include some survey sessions on "What silly traditions around here ought to go?"

34

How Do You Handle Hostility?

"Shut up, that's enough out of both of you." Words of a dad, coming up with a most unusual technique for handling hostility.

They call this dad's invention "Wednesday Night Is Mad Night." It started one day when he came home tired from the office. As he opened the front door, he heard his teenage daughter having it out with her mom. Both of them yelling full volume.

"I'd had all I could take that day," he said. "So I yelled at the top of *my* lungs. 'Shut up, you two, that's enough out of both of you. Now you listen to me! Sit down, write it on a piece of paper and get it all out of your system.' Then I got a box, cut a hole in the top and issued this order, 'From now on, anytime anyone around here has a gripe against anyone, write it out, drop it in the box and then we'll discuss all these things on Wednesday.'

"Funny how this goes. Sometimes by Wednesday you can't remember what it was all about. Or if you do remember, it seems kind of silly. Of course, some battles do have to be settled right now. For sure, some kinds of hostility shouldn't wait even a few days. But I tell you, our little Wednesday box has made a big difference."

Questions for a family bull session: How do you handle hostility at your house? Bury it? Discuss it? Or let it do a slow burn till the fire flames and someone gets hurt? If "Mad" night wouldn't work with our tribe, could we come up with something better?

Open a magazine, read a newspaper, turn on the tube. Obviously some of the young have never been trained to let off steam respectably. In a society like ours there better be some strong feelings. Nobody should sit easy to social injustice, poverty, pollution or deceit in high places. But so many of the angry young go at it wrong. Is this because they weren't allowed to surface their feelings at home?

Here's a comment from a college girl with an unusual tribute to her parents. She writes, "The most loving thing my parents ever did was to let me hate them."

That could be worth a retake for my fathering. Am I operating under the delusion that my children ought to like me one-hundred percent of the time? Do we have some healthy outlets for hostility in our family? Have we included some training in how to surface the negatives? Would it improve things around here if I could be loving enough to let them hate me?

35.

Early Training for Money Management

What would you do if you had all the money in the world?

Would you save it? Give some away? Start a few interesting projects? Have fun? Travel?

What got me on this is the far-out comment of a funny man. When his friend asked, "What would you do if you had all the money in the world?" he quipped, "I'd take it and apply it on my debts just as far as it would go."

Most of us can say, "Amen. Me too." Money can be a drag. Or it can be fun, excitement, a real pleasure. And the difference may begin early.

So here are some questions strictly for dads:

Are my children at an age where we should be having some sessions on money matters?

Should I be teaching them about budgets, bills and bookkeeping; spending, saving, giving; time payments, monthly payments, interest payments?

Reasonable questions, aren't they? And if I'm the one to do this job, where do we begin? Well, here's one solid rock for money education in our fathering— My child, your child, any child understands the value of a dollar best by managing his own dollar!

So here's the actual account of one family who built on that. When they began, they didn't have much money. But they wanted their children to learn from what they did have. That's why they decided to gradually transfer the children's expenditures into the children's hands. Spelled out it read like this:

"By your junior year in high school, your allowance will cover everything except the food you eat and the roof over your head. You prepare your own budget, listing your total needs. Clothes, cokes, haircuts; telephone, toiletries, dates; school, shows, recreation; gasoline, gifts, miscellaneous. Include in it something to give and something to save. You know we believe in work, so whatever you earn can apply against your allowance. Or you can save that for college, for marriage, for something big we agree on. We'll work with you at first but by the time you finish high school, you'll be an expert at handling money."

Daring? Foolish to trust a child that much? Maybe it isn't. I've been recommending this a long time and I know any number of families who do it. Which makes it easy for me to ask some of the young set how they see it.

Two quotes:

First, from a high school boy—"As long as you are spending your folk's money, you might not care all that much. But when it's your own money, you really think." Quote two from a college daughter—"I think if more parents would do this, they wouldn't have to worry so much later. Besides, our friends are always telling us how lucky we are to have parents like that. So we really do appreciate them more."

36

Saturday Is Candy Day

What do you do about candy? How do you regulate the sweet tooth?

A California mother writes, "My husband believes we should never allow our children to have candy, and I mean absolutely never. He has ordered me to see that they never do. I think he's being unreasonable. It seems that we get along fine on the big things. But it's little things like this that make for such ugly feelings between us. Any advice you can give us? We sure need help."

I'm glad she wrote because I know a couple with an interesting thing going. Only before we get to them, let's pick up on her word "ordered." The smart dad doesn't "order" people. Good fathering finds a better way.

Same thing goes for absolute denial. Those things with an "absolutely never" tag may become more attractive than they really are.

So here's about the couple:

Vincent and Karen have two little girls who like candy. Lots of it. Often. Their little girls also have a grandpa and grandma who have a tough time saying "No." To handle the problem, Vincent and Karen have a gimmick called "Saturday is candy day." What this means is that their girls can eat candy on Saturday only.

That, it seems to me, is one smart handling of a difficult problem. To which most dentists would say, "Hallelujah." (I hear from them, too.)

Cutting down the sweet intake isn't the only plus for "candy day." It also makes for good self discipline. Each little girl has a sack in the cupboard where she stores her horde all week. Grandpa's and grandma's candy goes there along with the chewing gum.

That's got to be good.

These girls have something special to look forward to on Saturday. Life is more exciting for all of us if there's some anticipation in it. So that's another plus for "candy day."

Their mother says it's also great in the grocery store, when they have company, or any time the kids begin to make demands.

But that isn't all.

Karen and Vincent say: "Since we started 'Saturday is candy day,' our girls even seem to ration themselves on Saturday."

Smart parenting. This young father and mother have taken a loser and made it a winner. They've turned a negative into a positive.

"No, you can't."

"Yes, you can. On Saturday."

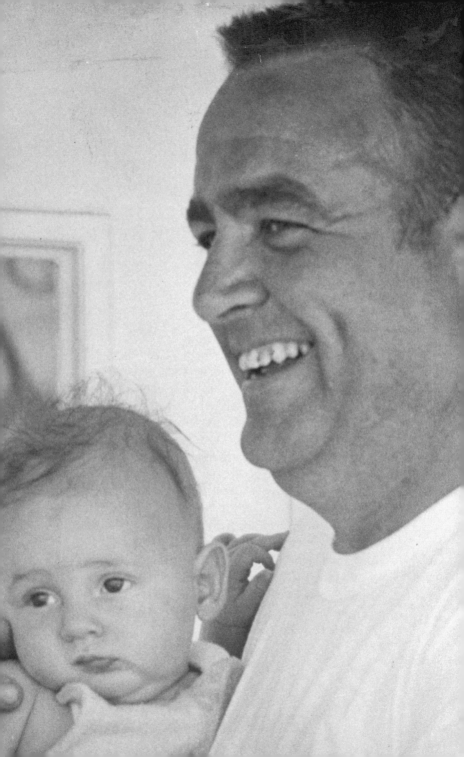

37.

Paul Is a Five O'Clock Riser

Paul is a five o'clock riser. Every morning, same song, next verse: "Here I am, world. Let's get a move on."

That might be all right in some families. But Paul has four brothers and sisters. With a gang like that their mother needs her sleep. Plus a hard-working dad could do with some extra shuteye.

Yet every morning there he is! Six years of zip, zam, and zowie, ready to go at 5:00 A.M.

Question: How do you handle these souped-up young fry?

Paul's mom and dad have learned some things which won't get the job done. Like trying to fool the clock inside their hyperactive celebrator of life. When you're into this particular effort, you let him stay up late. Get him groggy enough so he'll sack in later in the morning. But it was a bomb. Every day there he was "bright-eyed and bushy-tailed."

Next they ran him through the various other gamuts of frenzied parenthood. They came down heavy with the threats—"You better stay in bed or else." Same effect: zero. As a follow-up to that turkey, they took away privileges, which is a very good procedure sometimes—"Unless you stay in bed till 7:00, you can't ride your bicycle." "Can't watch television." "We'll put away your skates for a whole week." You guessed it. That didn't work either. So, like desperate moms and dads will do, they resorted at last to pleading, begging, whining.

Then the light at the end of their tunnel. One night driving home from work, Paul's dad had an inspiration. He's a strong man at the company. Especially adept at handling people. He majored in psychology and he's done well with it.

One of the principles he goes by is this basic: "The more liberty we give our employees, the better. If we can let them do it their way, they'll do a better job for us."

So that night driving home he asked himself: "Is there any possible way we can make friends with this early riser inside Paul? Why not let the little guy get up at 5:00 A.M.? Couldn't he be taught to make his own hot chocolate? Maybe with us off his back, he'd leave the bedroom quietly, go to the den, let in the dog, study his home work. Nobody telling him anything for two hours every morning. Bet he'd go for that, big!"

He did!

38

Should We Teach Our Children to Fight Back?

What should we teach our children about fighting? I mean about fighting back.

This Michigan mother and father are having an argument. Obviously, it isn't anything like a knock-down, drag-out affair. They're the gentle kind. But their disagreement is serious enough to call for a letter.

Their Jeremy is one of those nice little boys who wouldn't harm anyone. No sissy, but he'd never pick a fight. That's not Jeremy's style.

Enter Tubby.

Tubby is the school bully. He beats up kids just because they're standing around. And he considers it a bad day if he hasn't clobbered someone. Since Jeremy doesn't go for fighting, Tubby really zeroes in on him. Guess he sees him as a kind of a nice punching bag for warmups.

Jeremy's mother writes:

I'm a pacifist. That's how my parents raised me. They taught me it's wrong to fight, and I made my way through childhood just being nice to everybody. But my husband doesn't see it this way. He's always been the competitive kind. Big in athletics. So he taught Jeremy how to fight and I must say things have been a whole lot better for Jeremy. Only I still wonder.

Most of us dads can turn on some switches in our history and get the picture. "Fake a punch with his hand. Deliver a wallop with the other. Practice. Practice. Get it down pat."

Then the inevitable happened. Tubby jumped Jeremy just once too often. This time Jeremy let him have it, and "lo, how the mighty hath fallen." Let's hope the girls in his class were there, and the guys too, to see him flatten Tubby.

Still here's his mother's question. Should a father teach his son to fight?

She's asking some other important questions in her letter. Questions like, "What will it do to Jeremy later? What if he meets someone so much stronger he can't possibly handle him physically?"

Certain letters seem loaded for trouble. They want us to take sides, especially theirs. So fire away, all you gentle mothers, because I'm about to put in with Jeremy's dad.

You know and I know that fighting isn't the final answer to everything. But it isn't right either to let any child be bullied around.

Sometimes a left hook and a right cross are exactly what's needed for better relationships.

39

Husband, Father and Semi-Driver

Bob drives a semi. Drives it every ten days from Kenosha, Wisconsin to the West Coast. A big, red, white and blue semi.

Inside, his cab is clean as your living room. Tender loving care keeps it that way. Bob keeps it that way because he almost always has one member of his family with him.

This time it was his wife, Jean. She's how we got the story. My wife and I sat down beside her in a restaurant north of San Diego. Beautiful little restaurant with lousy service. We sat, sipping coffee at the counter, and started talking. She asked where we were from and vice versa. Then she took off about Bob. He was out that morning loading up for the trip back to Kenosha. Coming west he hauls dry cargo—floor wax, paper products, soap from Chicago. Going back it's perishables—California produce.

We asked her how often she made the trip with him. "Oh, real often," she answered, her dark eyes snapping. "This time I left the kids with my folks. We're having a ball. One day we spent three hours with a couple in Sidney, Nebraska. Never met them before. Bob has a citizens' band radio and they've been talking for three years. We do a lot of things like this. Meet some interesting people. Sometimes we sleep in the truck and when we feel like a shower, we stay in a motel. They have special rates for truckers. Did you know that?"

So she went on and on singing her hymn of praise for her trucker and life. (And—hallelujah—we finally got some service.)

Then I asked her the inimitable question: "How can a man travel every ten days from Kenosha to the West Coast and still be a good father?"

"Oh, Bob is the very best," she said. "When he is home, you should see the way the kids spend all their time with him. Drop everything to be there. They think he's the greatest. Maybe it's partly because every trip he takes one of the kids with him. He even takes them out of school. We think they can get educated lots of different ways. He's teaching our fourteen-year-old to handle the truck. And when his legs get a little longer, I bet he'll get hooked like his dad. Bob is absolutely crazy about his job. Says he'll never try anything else."

Well, it was some session there in that little restaurant. Beautiful. She talked about their hibachi and the steaks they cook at the roadside parks; about the places they swim, the shows they see. Then she added, "I think I'm so lucky to be married to such a wonderful man."

I hear many mothers complain their husbands are gone so much. Then here's Jean with a husband who travels every ten days from Kenosha to the West Coast, and she is saying, "I think we're lucky."

Well, I do too.

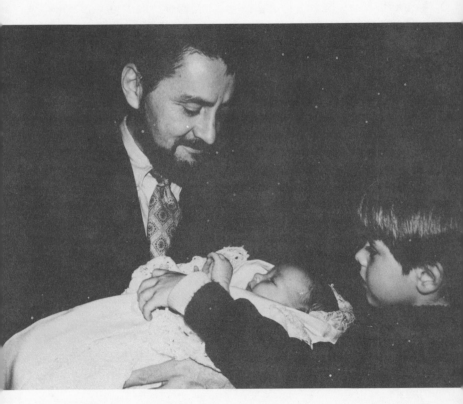

"God Is Like My Father?"

Comes now a real heavy and it's strictly for dads. I first heard this at the board meeting of a psychiatric hospital. Though I'm not a shrink, they had me there for a good reason. I represented those places where religion and psychiatry might work together.

This particular day we were listening to a famous child psychiatrist read his paper on "Theological Implications in the Father-Child Relationship."

He began by saying that he himself was a father, and he'd been doing an unusual survey. Then he socked it to us with this announcement: "No little child will think more of God than he thinks of his father!"

That really came down hard on me. In fact, it came down so hard I decided to check it out. I work with parents, teen-agers, the college set. I've spent hours with alcoholics, drug users, unhappy marriages. People of every kind with problems. I rap with them

121

often. So I can ask questions. That's where it came clear—the man is right!

All this negative input takes place early for a tricky reason. A little child can't contrast. For a long time he can only compare. We teach him to pray "Our Father who art in heaven." And we tell him "God is our Heavenly Father."

See now what happens. In his child mind he muses: "God is like my father? I'm not so sure my father really cares much about me. He's always playing golf, watching television, reading the newspaper. Besides he isn't very nice to my mother. He's not even fair. I don't think I'd like God."

So what can we do?

Here's one possibility for the dad with enough humility to get it done. It's a little speech to the kids. Early.

"Listen to me troops. Where I'm the kind of father I should be, that's what God is like! Where I am not so hot, I hope you'll learn the all-important process of contrast. Wherever the Bible says that God is like a father, you can understand it means that God is like a perfect father. You know I'm not perfect. But I'm going to keep on trying. And I want you to know that I know I've got a long way to go."

So here's a hearty thanks to the child psychiatrist for his hard and heavy needle. From what I've seen in my own family and out of my personal survey, that was one smart dad.

Acknowledgments

The story of Warren and his mother's over-push for honesty (Chapter 31: The Big Lion) is taken from Dr. Shedd's book *Promises to Peter: Building a Bridge from Parents to Child*, Word Publishing Co. Copyright © Charlie W. Shedd & The Abundance Foundation, 1970.

PHOTO CREDITS

Photo on pages 12, 40, 67, and 99

by Jean-Claude LeJuene.

Photo on page 16

by Jim Hunt.

Photo on page 24

by Religious News Service.

Photo on page 29

by Orville Andrews.

Photos on pages 31 and 63

by Molly Barrett.

Photos on pages 48, 50 and 91

by Eugene Geissler.

Photos on pages 55, 56 and 81

by Beth Slatery.

Photos on pages 70, 108, 111 and 116

by Patrick Slatery.

Photos on pages 75 and 77

by Vernon Sigl.

Photos on pages 87 and 105

by Anthony F. Rowland.

Photos on pages 94 and 114

by Marne Breckensick Photo.

Photo on page 120

by Charlie Jones.

Dr. Charlie Shedd, author of the nationally syndicated column "Strictly for Dads," is a Presbyterian minister, speaker, writer and father of five children. He was born in Cedar Rapids, Iowa, where he received both his B.A. degree and D.Litt. degree from Coe College. He received his Bachelor of Divinity degree from McCormick Seminary in Chicago and his Doctor of Divinity degree from Hastings College in Nebraska. As hobbies Dr. Shedd enjoys woodworking and traveling. He has conducted several seminars for writers throughout the United States and now conducts Family Life Forums.

He has published many books including *The Stork is Dead* and *Letters to Philip*. His book *Letters to Karen* sold over one million copies. Dr. Shedd and his family live on Jekyll Island, Georgia.